For Ian – M.B.

For everyone who's curious – C.W.

First published 2022 by Walker Books Ltd,
87 Vauxhall Walk, London SE11 5HJ

This edition published 2024

2 4 6 8 10 9 7 5 3 1

Text © 2022 Moira Butterfield

Illustrations © 2022 Cindy Wume

The right of Moira Butterfield and Cindy Wume to be identified as author and illustrator respectively of this work has been asserted in accordance with the Copyright, Designs and Patents Act 1988

This book has been typeset in AnkeSans

Printed in China

All rights reserved. No part of this book may be reproduced, transmitted or stored in an information retrieval system in any form or by any means, graphic, electronic or mechanical, including photocopying, taping and recording, without prior written permission from the publisher.

British Library Cataloguing in Publication Data:
a catalogue record for this book is available from the British Library

ISBN 978-1-5295-1509-1

www.walker.co.uk

THIS WALKER BOOK BELONGS TO:

_____

_____

_____

MY BIG BOOK OF QUESTIONS ABOUT THE WORLD

Moira Butterfield   illustrated by Cindy Wume

WALKER BOOKS
AND SUBSIDIARIES
LONDON · BOSTON · SYDNEY · AUCKLAND

POP!
Questions pop into our heads all the time, every day, about the world and the starry sky.

WHY?

HOW?

WHAT?

OUR WORLD

WHAT IS THE WORLD?

The world is a watery, rocky place, floating in space.

It looks like a cloudy blue and green marble.

The Moon is like a grey pebble circling round it.

We sometimes call it the Earth ...

and we also call it home.

WHAT'S THE WORLD MADE OF?

The world is made of layers, like a chocolate-covered lolly with ice cream and toffee in the middle.

It has a thick outside layer of rock called the "crust". That's what we're all standing on now.

Next comes a layer of rock so hot that the lower part has melted and become runny like sauce. After that is another layer of runny metal, so hot it flows like gooey syrup.

In the middle there's a big solid ball of metal that's unbelievably, scorchingly hot – which means the heart of the world is glowing!

WHAT SHAPE IS THE WORLD?

The world is round, but not like a ball. It's flatter at the top and bottom, and fatter around the middle — more like a grapefruit. Imagine you are a giant, touching the Earth with your fingers: you would feel high mountains and deep valleys, flat fields and wiggly rivers.

HOW WIDE IS THE WORLD?

It would take about two days to fly round the world, under a month to drive and years to walk. So many steps, so much to see!

The world measures 40,075 kilometres around its middle, which we call the "equator". The equator isn't a "real" line — it's like an imaginary belt around the world's tummy.

40,075 km

HOW FAR AWAY IS THE MOON?

The Moon is our neighbour, but it's really far away — hundreds of thousands of kilometres, in fact. It would take about three days to get there by speedy space rocket, or six months if you could drive in a space car (without stopping for a rest).

But sometimes, when the Moon is bright, it gets reflected in a puddle, as if it tumbled from the sky and splashed down by your feet.

The Moon is a rocky, dusty place. The dark patches you can sometimes see on it are areas of especially dark rock.

THE LAND AROUND US

WHAT'S THE HIGHEST MOUNTAIN?

Mount Everest is the highest mountain on Earth.

It's a fearsome, freezing, snowy place of jagged crags and icy cliffs.

It reaches as high in the sky as aeroplanes fly.

Everest is 8,848 metres high. If you stood at the top you would see more mountains all around you, stretching as far as your eyes could see. Together these mountains are called the Himalayas.

WHERE'S THE BIGGEST FOREST?

The boreal forest is the biggest. It stretches for mile after mile, like a long scarf of fir trees wrapped around the far north of our planet.

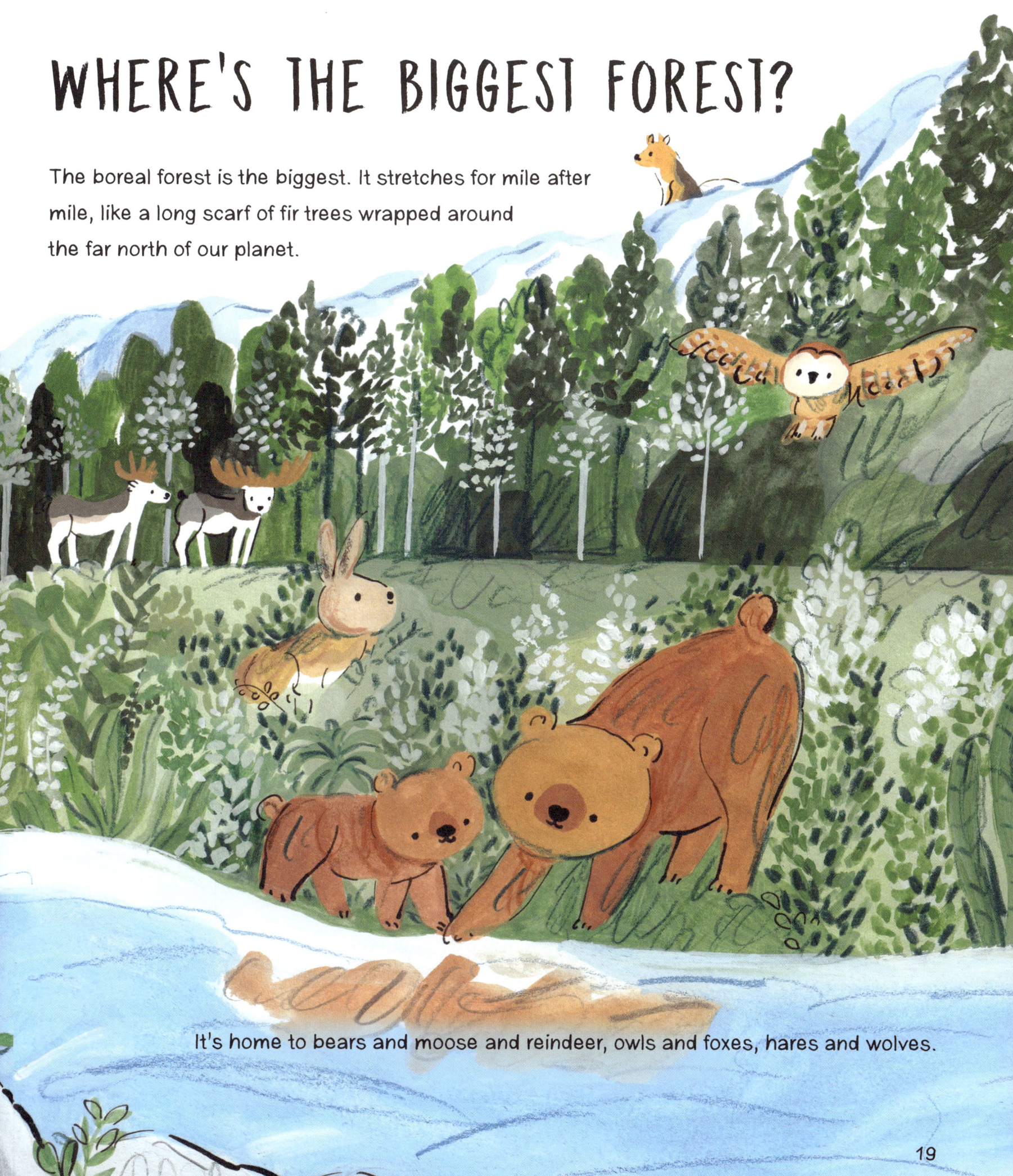

It's home to bears and moose and reindeer, owls and foxes, hares and wolves.

WHERE'S THE HOTTEST PLACE?

Death Valley is the hottest spot. It's as hot as an oven that's baking cookies.

If you stood on its bare, dry rocks,
hot air would rise up all around you and
make things look wobbly as you watched.

Death Valley is in California, USA. Although it's very hot, birds and snakes live there. So do desert tortoises and sheep with big curly horns.

WHERE'S THE COLDEST PLACE?

Antarctica is the coldest place on Earth. It's in the far south of the world.

It gets colder than a freezer and if you went in the clothes you normally wear, you'd very quickly sh ... sh ... shiver. Soon you'd be f-f-frozen like a sn-sn-snowman.

If you were standing at the North Pole you would be in the Arctic, at the northernmost spot in the world.

If you were standing at the South Pole you would be in Antarctica, at the southernmost spot in the world.

WHAT'S UNDERGROUND?

Soil, home to wiggly worms ...

roots from plants, like underground knitting ...

stones small enough to squeeze in your hand and stretches of rock so big and wide we call them rock beds ...

pipes that carry gurgling water ...

lost jewellery ...

ancient bone ...

wires that buzz with electricity ...

broken china ...

buried treasure ...

gold and silver ...

and even diamonds.

WHO LIVES AT THE SOUTH POLE?

Penguins live near the South Pole but not the North. Polar bears live near the North Pole but not the South. Humans visit both.

Penguins don't mind the super-strong winds at the South Pole.

Polar bears don't mind the floating icebergs around the North Pole.

Animals live everywhere! They're even in the thickest, most jungly jungles.

THE SEA

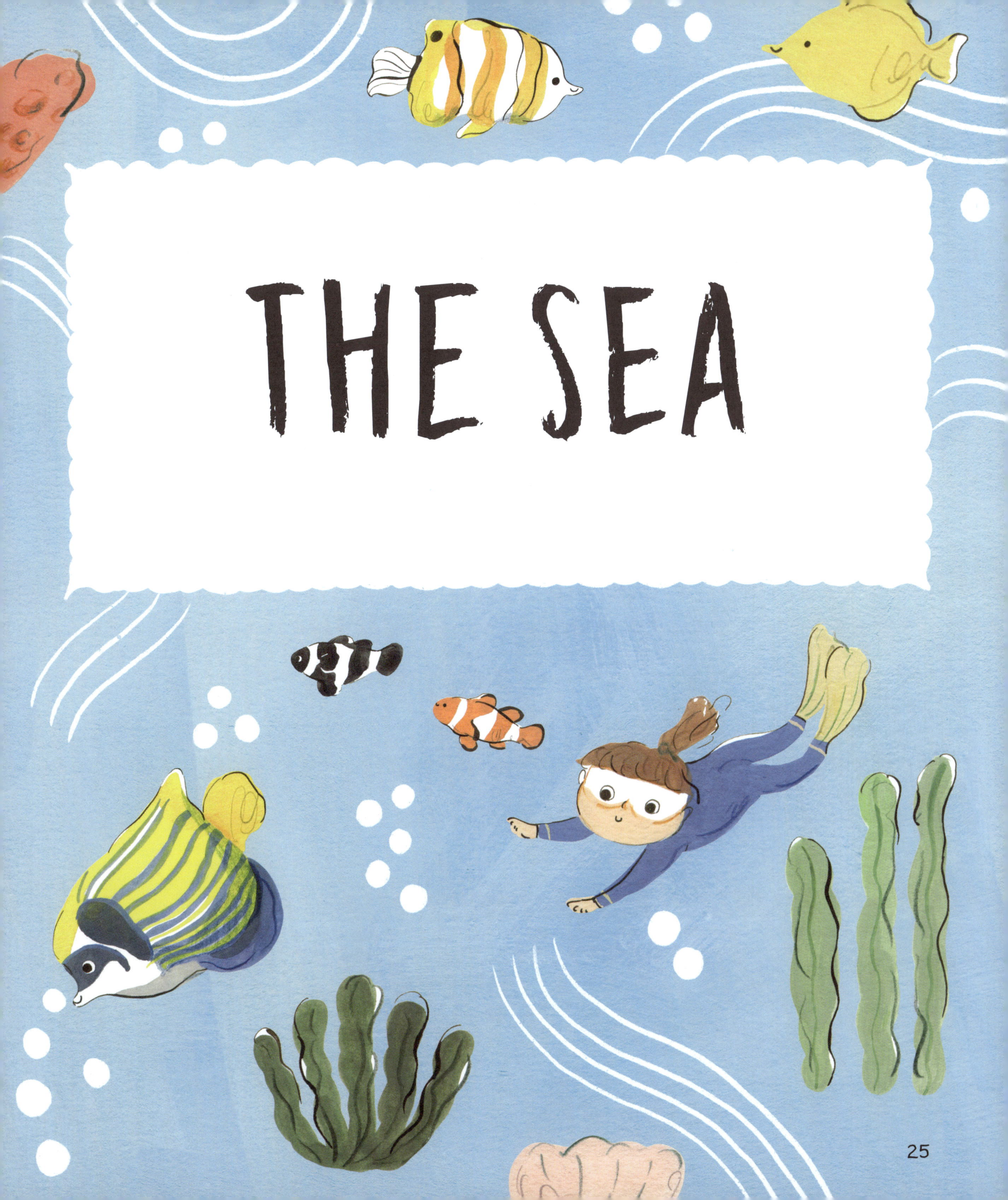

WHAT IS THE SEA?

Sea is salty water flowing around the world, round the beaches and the cliffs, round the rocks and the fishing boats.

It would flow around your toes, too, if you dipped them in and wiggled them.

On maps we split the world's seawater into five giant sections that we call oceans — the Arctic, the Southern, the Pacific, the Atlantic and the Indian.

WHAT IS A WAVE?

A wave is water pushing along, moving up and down like a wavy snake.

Breaking wave

Wind blows → Waves gets bigger

The wind blows the water into waves across the salty surface of the sea. Sometimes softly, sometimes strongly until the waves stretch up tall and curl like your fingers bending over. Then ... CRASH! They hit the shore and spread around — like your fingers stretching wide!

The biggest wave that anyone ever surfed stretched over 24 metres tall: as high as a tower block.

WHY IS THE SEA SALTY?

Sea salt comes from the rocks of the world. Over time, water washes up against them, slapping them, rubbing them, cracking and crumbling them.

The salt from the rocks mixes into the water — if you go swimming in the sea, you might taste it on your tongue. It's the taste of the ocean!

River water has a little bit of salt in it, but not enough to taste.

All the rivers run into the seas, taking their salt with them. That's why the seas are saltier.

WHAT'S AT THE BOTTOM OF THE SEA?

The bottom of the sea looks different around the world. In some places there are reefs of branching corals, home to lots of tiny fish; in others, there are rocks and slippery seaweed (a good hiding place for crabs). In deep parts of the sea there are flat fields of mud: fish with flashing lights swim here, which light up the darkness like decorations. There are even mountains on the seabed, as high as mountains on the land, and there are very, very deep trenches, far below.

The deepest part of the ocean is called the Mariana Trench.
It is so deep that Mount Everest, the highest mountain on land, would fit inside easily.

PLANTS

HOW MANY DIFFERENT PLANTS ARE THERE?

There are thousands of different plants — smooth, spiky, smelly, frilly, stripy, spotty, sticky, juicy and sometimes delicious!

We know about nearly 400,000 different types of plants in the world but there are probably lots more we haven't discovered yet.

WHAT DO PLANTS EAT?

A plant makes its own food, but first it needs some ingredients, just like you would if you were baking a cake.

1. Warm sunlight and gas from the air come in through its leaves.
2. Water and minerals (goodness) from the soil come up through its roots.

When it has what it needs it makes sugary watery plant food to help it grow ... and **grow** ... and **grow**!

carbon dioxide (CO_2)

oxygen (O_2)

water + minerals

Every minute of every day, plants are helping us to breathe. When they make their food, they also make a gas called oxygen and send it back out into the air. We humans need oxygen when we breathe in — so take a breath and say *thank you* to the plants!

WHAT ARE FLOWERS FOR?

Flowers make seeds that scatter around, to one day grow into new plants. Animals help them: a fuzzy buzzy bee will do.

1. The flower makes a drink called nectar. It makes tiny grains of pollen, too.

2. When the bee comes to drink the nectar, pollen dust sticks on its back.

3. The bee flies to another flower and the pollen falls off its hairy bristles.

4. To make new seeds, flowers must get pollen from other flowers like them.

By carrying the pollen around, the bee does a great job. Bzzzzz!

Birds, bats, butterflies and beetles help to carry pollen, too.

WHAT IS THE BIGGEST PLANT?

Trees are the biggest plants of all. Some of them grow as wide as towers and as tall as city office blocks. You'd need to use ropes to climb the biggest, as if you were mountain climbing.

The tallest tree that we know of is a redwood growing in California, USA. It towers over 116 metres high. It has its own name: Hyperion.

The biggest tree overall is not the tallest, but it is the heaviest. It's a giant sequoia tree growing in California. Its name is General Sherman and it weighs around 1.9 million kilograms: roughly the same as 130 big trucks.

WHAT IS THE SMALLEST PLANT?

Duckweed is the smallest plant. Each leaf is tinier than a grain of rice.

You'll see lots of it spreading over ponds, like a green rug thrown on the water. Ducks dip their beaks down to grab a mouthful.

WHY DO LEAVES SOMETIMES CHANGE COLOUR?

In winter, some trees get rid of their leaves, then grow new ones in spring. When the leaves start to die, the ingredients inside them begin to change: that's why they turn from summery green to the colours of a flickering fire... Before floating down like papery notes, to go dry and crunchy under your boots.

ANIMALS

HOW MANY ANIMALS ARE THERE?

There are so many animals in the world that we can't count them exactly, but we do know what *kinds* of creatures there are...
Reptiles, such as scaly snakes; insects, such as buzzing bees; fishes, such as darting minnows; birds, such as silvery owls; and mammals, such as you and me.
There are several other kinds as well, such as snails, frogs and wiggly worms. How many *kinds* of animals are there, altogether?
A planetful!

There are probably about 8 million different kinds of animals in the world altogether, though nobody knows for sure.

WHAT DO ANIMALS DO ALL DAY?

Some are busy looking for food.
Some are building homes to live in.
Some are looking after their babies.
Some are resting. They'll wake at night.
Some are hopping, flying, swimming...
And one is reading this book
right now.

DO ANIMALS GO TO SLEEP?

Every animal rests sometimes.

If you're a hamster – in a nest.

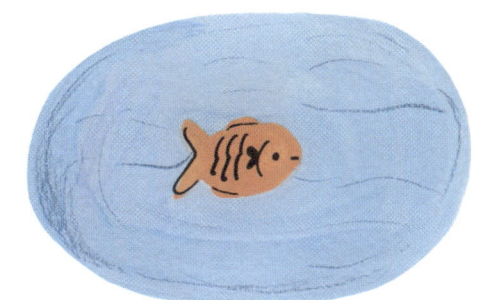

If you're a fish – while swimming along.

If you're a fox – in an earthy den.

If you're a bat – upside-down.

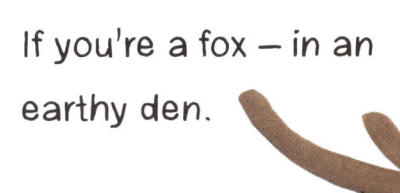

If you're a horse – while standing up.

If you're you – snuggling in your bed.

Koalas are the sleepiest animals of all, and are only awake for about two hours every day.

45

DO ANIMALS TALK TO EACH OTHER?

Creatures send each other messages in lots of different ways.

Koalas bellow.

Lots of birds tweet, but ostriches boom.

Dolphins click and squeak and whistle.

Crocodiles chirp!

DO ANIMALS PLAY GAMES?

All kinds of animals play games, especially when they're young.

Lambs leap and kick their hooves.

Puppies wrestle.

Kittens roll.

Horses gallop in the wind.

Nothing's more fun than chasing a tail, or batting a stick, or pretending to fight but not really hurting, and then, at the end, being friends.

WHAT'S THE BIGGEST ANIMAL?

The blue whale glides like a submarine through the oceans.

It's as long as five African elephants in a line, or two big buses in a queue.

It's bigger than dinosaurs ever were, but gentle as a parent with a baby.

Blue whales swim in all of the world's oceans. They can call to each other through the water with a sound that's louder than a jet plane, and are able to hear each other across hundreds of kilometres.

WHAT ARE THE SMALLEST ANIMALS?

Microfauna (*my-crow-for-na*).
They float in the water or wriggle in the soil,
as tiny as specks of dust.

They look like mini shrimps or spiders,
or just funny blobs with legs
and curly tails and bristly heads.

Microfauna are so tiny you would need a microscope to see them.

There are probably millions of different kinds but nobody knows how many there are for sure.

WHAT ARE BABY ANIMALS CALLED?

A baby bird is a chick.

A baby elephant is a calf.

A baby bear is a cub.

A baby porcupine is a... Um... Er...
Wait a minute... Here it is:
a porcupette. Perfect!

PEOPLE

HOW MANY PEOPLE ARE THERE IN THE WORLD?

There are 8 billion people on the Earth. If we all held hands and stood in a line, we would stretch around the planet hundreds of times.

WHY DO PEOPLE LOOK DIFFERENT FROM EACH OTHER?

Humans look different in many ways: we have lots of shapes and sizes and faces and hair and clothes and ways of speaking.

We're like the paint colours in a picture: it's a good thing that we are all different, because – together – it makes us amazing!

HOW DO PEOPLE SAY HELLO?

There are lots of languages in the world, so there are lots of ways to say hello.

There are around 6,500 languages in the world. That's a lot of ways to say hello!

WHAT ARE PEOPLE MADE OF?

All kinds of things make up a human: bones that give your body its shape (otherwise you'd look like jelly); skin to hold your bits inside you; blood travelling round your body; a heart to pump your blood around; a brain, so you can think....

BRAIN: It sends signals to the rest of your body to tell it what to do.

HEART: It pumps all the time.

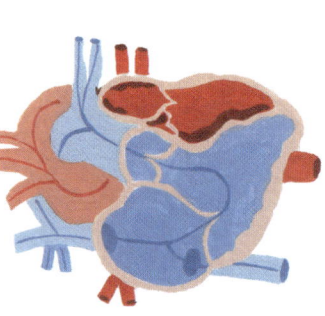

BONES: There are usually 206 of them in an adult.

SKIN: It's waterproof, like a very useful raincoat.

BLOOD: It carries round things your body needs, such as oxygen.

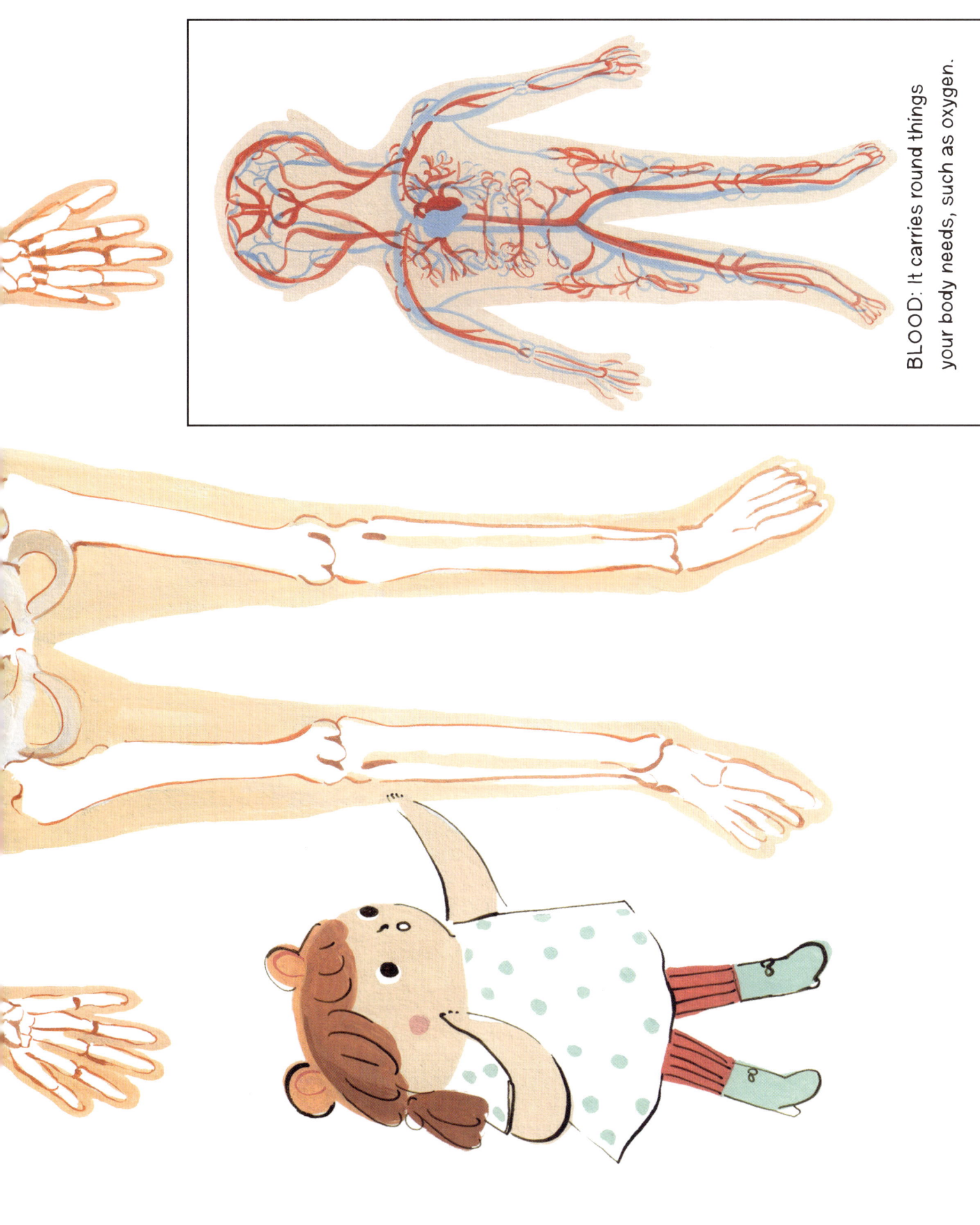

And that (with your other knobbly, hairy, squashy, bendy, ticklish parts) is you!

WHAT ARE PEOPLE GOOD AT?

We humans can't run as fast as a cheetah,
or fly like a bird, or climb like a spider.
But we can do many, many things...
Some of us sing.
Some play music.
Some of us dance.
Some of us draw.
Some of us invent.
Some play sports.
Some of us build
and some of us mend.
Some of us even go into space.
One of the best things we can ALL
do is be kind to each other.
We can do that every day!

THE WEATHER

WHAT IS THE SKY MADE OF?

The sky is made of air. It has water mist in it, too, and tiny flecks of floating dust.
The sky wraps around you and stretches up ... up ... up ... above the highest mountain, all the way to space.
That's where the air ends.

Wind is the air moving: whirling and swirling, and blowing your hat off!

Air is made of "gases". The gases are made of teeny-tiny parts called "molecules". You can't see the molecules but you can feel them moving if you blow on the back of your hand.

WHAT ARE CLOUDS MADE OF?

Clouds are made of water mist: they change shape when the wind blows.

Cloud shapes have names. Here are two to spot.

CUMULONIMBUS: piled up in the sky. Sometimes they might bring rain.

CUMULUS: drifting puffy white clouds.

Sometimes clouds look like real things ... like a hat, a fish or a horse, perhaps!

WHAT MAKES IT RAIN ...

1. Tiny drops of water mist drift up from rivers and seas.
2. They bump together inside a cloud and join to make bigger drops.
3. The drops get too heavy to float. They fall out of the cloud as rain.

... OR THUNDER?

Thunder is the noise that happens when lightning zips down to the ground.
In its super-hot, sizzling path, the air EXPLODES and makes the sound!

Lightning is made in the clouds when water droplets and bits of ice bump together, and make electricity.
The lightning is a super-fast line of electricity that shoots out of the clouds.

... OR SNOW?

When it gets very cold (shivery, freezing, wintery cold),
water in the clouds turns into ice: tiny pieces of ice called crystals.
The ice crystals stick to dust in the air, and clump together to make snowflakes.

The snowflakes grow heavy, then fall from the sky,
turning the ground glittery white.

WHY IS THE SKY BLUE?

On a lovely sunny day, sunlight turns the sky blue. The sunlight is made of different colours mixed together like paint on a plate: there's red, orange, yellow and green, indigo (a blueish purple), violet (like the flowers), and, of course, blue, too.
Blue! Blue! Beautiful blue!

When sunlight streams towards the Earth, it bounces on the "molecules" in the air, then it splits into different colours, scattering in all directions. Which colour scatters the most? Which colour washes the sky?
Blue! Blue! Beautiful blue!

Sometimes, at sunrise and sunset, the light scatters differently and the sky turns red and orange.

WHAT IS A RAINBOW?

Sometimes, when the sun shines through raindrops, we can SEE the sunlight colours. The raindrops are like tiny mirrors: they split the light into seven stripes, and then a rainbow appears in the sky ... a glowing arch of sparkling sun.

OUT IN

SPACE

WHAT'S IN SPACE?

The Sun, a massive blazing star:
it's made of burning, churning gases.

The other stars: they're all massive too,
but from here they look like dots.

Planets: they go around the stars.
Our planet, Earth, goes around the Sun.

Moons: they go around the planets.
Earth has a moon of its own.

A lot of other floating stuff...
rocks and ice, clouds
of dust... Oh, and
miles and miles
of nothing. There's
lots and lots of
space in Space.

WHAT LIVES IN SPACE?

Could there be monsters made of jelly, with lots of legs and several eyes, or perhaps people just like us, but with glowing heads and bright blue ears? We haven't found any yet, but there's a lot of space left to explore — so we can't say for sure!

WHY DOES THE SUN RISE AND SET?

The Sun seems to rise in the morning and sink down at evening-time.

Long ago, people thought it was pulled across the sky by horses...

But it's not really the Sun that's moving: it's the Earth. It's us!

WHERE DO STARS GO IN THE DAYTIME?

Stars don't go anywhere – they're shining brightly day and night. You just can't see them when the sky is light!

On a clear night it's possible to see lots of stars from Earth. Scientists can see even more by looking through a space telescope, which shows up stars that are further away.

WHY DOES THE SKY GO DARK AT NIGHT?

The Earth is floating around the Sun: its journey takes it one whole year. As it travels, it spins around — one spin takes a day and a night.

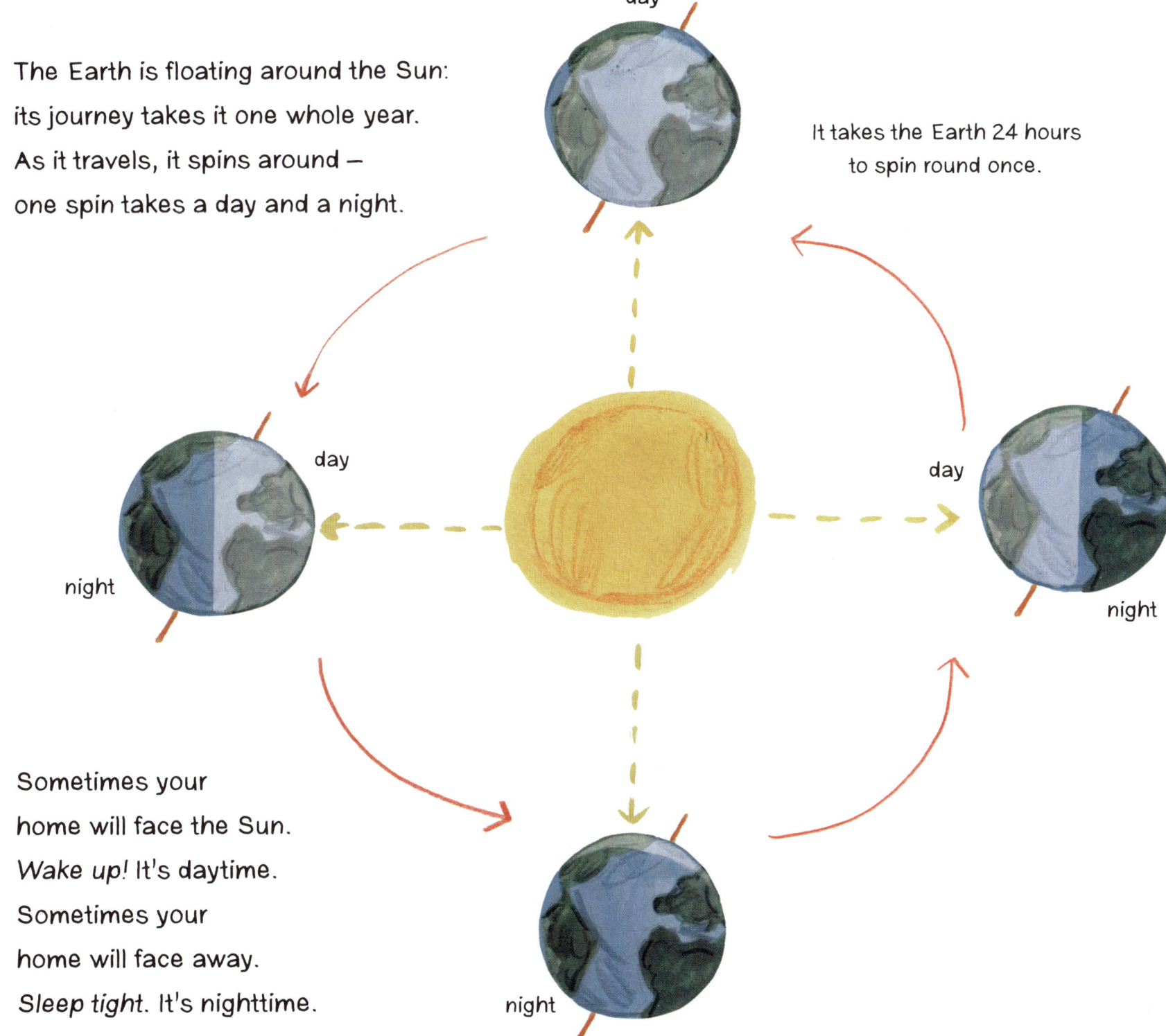

It takes the Earth 24 hours to spin round once.

Sometimes your home will face the Sun. *Wake up!* It's daytime. Sometimes your home will face away. *Sleep tight.* It's nighttime.

We can't feel the Earth spinning because we're all travelling round with it, at the same speed.

WHAT DOES SPACE SMELL LIKE?

Astronauts say space smells like metal,
a little bit like a nail or a saucepan.
We know some planets have smelly gases,
like vinegar mixed with rotten eggs.
We also know what spaceships smell like...
Stinky, smelly astronauts!

WHAT DOES SPACE FEEL LIKE?

Walking in space feels like floating,
so astronauts train in swimming pools.
Next time you go for a swim,
put on your armbands so you can float
then imagine you're an astronaut.
"Mission control. Can you hear me?
I'm stepping outside. I'm moving in space!"

The first human went into space in 1961. His name was Yuri Gagarin, and when he saw Earth for the first time he said it was wonderful.

CAN WE GO ON HOLIDAY TO SPACE?

Not yet — but perhaps, one day, there might be a hotel on the Moon. There might not be beaches: only rocks. There might not be swimsuits: only spacesuits. But you would be able to see something really special ...

Planet Earth, outside your window.

POP!

Questions pop into our heads all the time, every day ...

but we also have some answers now.

I know what!

I know where!

I know why!

I know how!

Moira Butterfield is an internationally published children's author. She has written about a host of different subjects, from ancient treasures to future worlds via pirates, kings, jungles and sea monsters; her recent work includes *My Big Book of Transport* and *Grandma's Story*.

Cindy Wume is an illustrator and picture book maker based in Taiwan. She gained an MA in Children's Book Illustration at Cambridge School of Art in 2016. Her artworks have been twice selected for the Bologna Children's Book Fair Exhibition.